Contents

CHAPTER 1

Taylor speeds to stardom

Taylor Lautner revs the engine of a dirt bike. His muscles ripple under his black T-shirt and leather jacket. A pale girl with dark brown hair jumps on the back of the bike. With a glance at the angry vampire standing in the road, the pair speed away from Forks High School.

Five seconds later, Taylor puts the brakes on, and his co-star jumps off the bike. It's a **wrap**. Taylor is shooting a scene for *Eclipse*, the third film in the Twilight saga. He is in character as Jacob Black.

Taylor loves filming action scenes. It is his job to make the dangerous stunts, supernatural characters and romance seem real.

Before filming *Eclipse*, Taylor had never ridden a dirt bike. He took lessons and practised for two days. He wanted to prove that he could do his own stunt riding. Taylor didn't want a **stunt double** to stand in for any of Jacob's scenes. He only took two **takes** to get it right.

stunt double someone who performs action scenes in place of an actor

Although he practised hard, Taylor was nervous about shooting the dirt bike scene in *Eclipse*.

"I've never ridden a dirt bike before and yes, I rode the dirt bike for a total of five seconds in the film. But for those five seconds, I had to look as cool as possible."

Taylor on doing the stunts for *Eclipse* in an interview with *ComingSoon.net*.

Star Facts

Full name:
Taylor Daniel Lautner

Date of birth:
11 February 1992

Heritage: Taylor has French, Dutch, German and Native American **ancestors**

Pets: Roxy, a Maltese dog

Drives: a black BMW

Hobbies: jet skiing and fishing with his family

Favourite TV shows: *American Idol*; *So You Think You Can Dance?*

Fears: reptiles and sharks

Trademarks: huge smile; musclular body

Favourite sports: American football; karate

Worst habit: tapping his feet

Memorable moment: hiding from 2,000 screaming fans in a Brazilian hotel room

Describes himself as: friendly, outgoing, energetic and easy to talk to

Favourite line: "Does my being half naked bother you?"

"He's very set in his ways. But that is very informative of his personality. He's very steady. He has a really solid sense of himself."

Kristen Stewart describing her co-star Taylor, in an interview with *Rolling Stone* magazine

ancestors family members who lived long ago

Taylor showed off his sporting skills during a photo shoot for *Rolling Stone* magazine.

Taylor the athlete

Taylor is a natural athlete. As well as studying karate for seven years, he played American football and baseball for his school. Taylor's athletic ability helps him out on the dance floor, too. He has performed with hip-hop dance group LA Hip Kids, and jazz dance group Hot Shots. Taylor works hard to maintain the muscle he gained for the second Twilight film, *New Moon*.

child karate champion

Taylor was born into a normal family in Grand Rapids, Michigan, in the USA. His mum, Deborah, was a software developer, and his dad, Daniel, worked as an airline pilot. When Taylor was four, a fire burned down the family house. Luckily they were not at home. The Lautners settled into a new house in Hudsonville, Michigan. Taylor was six when his little sister, Makena, was born.

Soon after starting primary school, Taylor became interested in karate. The trips, flips and kicks came naturally to him. After just one year, Taylor won his first national tournament. At this tournament, he met world champion karate instructor Mike Chat, who would become his trainer.

At the age of eight, Taylor became a Junior World Champion. Karate was his life for the next few years, and by the time he was 12, Taylor had been Junior World Champion three times. Taylor's karate coach had connections with Hollywood filmmakers. He suggested that Taylor try out for a part in a Burger King advertisement. Taylor didn't get the part, but he caught the acting bug.

Taylor was one of the first members of the martial arts group XMA Performance Team.

Hollywood loved watching Taylor in action. He showed off his skills in films, on the red carpet, and on the show America's Most Talented Kids.

Taylor's big break

Taylor was soon signed up by an **agent**. He appeared in his first film in 2001, playing a ninja in *Shadow Fury*. However, Taylor's home was almost 2,000 miles (3,220 kilometres) from Hollywood. This made daily life tough. Sometimes, Taylor would get a call about an **audition** the following day. His family would take an early flight to Los Angeles. They had to fly back late on the same day, so that Taylor could go to school the next morning. Taylor also had to put up with teasing at school. Some pupils made fun of his acting. "I just had to tell myself I can't let this get to me," he remembers. "This is what I love to do. And I'm going to continue to do it."

To pursue a career in acting, Taylor needed to be closer to Hollywood. Taylor's parents told him that they would move to Los Angeles for a month. If he didn't get his big break after 30 days, they would move back to Michigan. Leaving friends and family behind was hard. But on the very last day of the trial month, Taylor got the callback he was waiting for. It gave him the confidence to continue acting.

"I'm definitely thankful to have a supportive family, I wouldn't have been able to do it without them."

Taylor speaking about his family in January 2011

Steady acting work

In Hollywood, Taylor won small roles on TV shows. He also did voice-over work for cartoons such as *What's New, Scooby Doo?* and *Duck Dodgers.* But Taylor really wanted to be on the big screen. He wanted to be a film star.

In 2005, Taylor tried out for the 3D film *The Adventures of Sharkboy and Lavagirl*. Taylor showed the director, Robert Rodriguez, his martial arts moves. Robert chose Taylor for the part immediately.

Taylor played Sharkboy, a superhero who was raised by sharks. Taylor was on **set** for three months in Austin, Texas. He had to study hard to keep up with his school work, but it was worth it. Taylor got to perform his own stunts. He even had the chance to **choreograph** some action scenes.

Sharkboy is a character from a dream, who was raised by sharks.

choreograph to design or plan a series of movements

The Adventures of Sharkboy and Lavagirl **premiered** in June 2005. Taylor, then aged 13, showed up in a denim jacket, ripped jeans, and unlaced shoes. He did more than pose on the red carpet. He pulled off acrobatic flips and leaps. The media loved his moves.

Playing Sharkboy even won Taylor some fans. "I'd be in the store, and boys would whisper to their mums," Lautner said in an interview. "Then the mums would say, 'Excuse me, are you Sharkboy?'"

Taylor didn't get star treatment at home. He studied hard and was a straight-A student at school. His parents asked him to do chores, and they gave him pocket money. Taylor still enjoyed normal things. He loved watching martial arts films such as *The Last Samurai*, and eating his favourite foods – steak with pepper sauce, and cake batter ice cream.

Since his role as Sharkboy, Taylor has been popular with the media.

In 2005, Taylor got a small part in the film *Cheaper by the Dozen 2*. The following year, he won a role on the TV show *Love, Inc*. He also did some more voice-over work. In 2008, Taylor appeared in *My Own Worst Enemy*, playing the son of Hollywood star Christian Slater. These were his last small roles. Taylor was about to land the role that would make him a superstar.

CHAPTER 3

Twilight approaches

In late 2007, filmmakers began searching for actors to appear in a film based on Stephenie Meyer's bestselling book, *Twilight*. They needed the right people to play characters that were loved by the book's millions of fans. In January 2008, an **open casting call** gave teenage boys a chance to try out for the role of Jacob Black, a friend of the main character, Bella Swan. Taylor hadn't even heard of *Twilight*. But his **agent** told him to give it a shot.

Taylor turned up early for his **audition**. He read lines with Kristen Stewart, who had already been cast as Bella. They read from the *Twilight* script and acted out scenes from the sequels, *New Moon* and *Eclipse*.

One month later, Taylor got a call. His dad, agent, and manager were all listening in. Together they learned that Taylor had won the part of Jacob Black. At 16, he would be *Twilight's* youngest star.

open casting call an audition where anyone is allowed to try out

Hundreds of fans greeted Taylor before *Twilight*'s US premiere.

Preparing for the role

Taylor began by reading *Twilight*, but not its sequels. Like his character, he didn't want to know what was in store. In the Twilight saga, Jacob is a member of the American Indian Quileute tribe. Taylor learned the tribe's legends and met some tribe members. He even learned to speak a little of their language.

Around the same time, Taylor decided that his career was causing him to miss too much school. He left secondary school early and began taking college courses instead. But he did go back to attend his high school prom (a dance for secondary school leavers), taking a friend as his date.

Taylor and his on-screen dad, Gil Birmingham (seated), had an instant connection.

EPHENIE MEYER

R OF THE #1 BESTSELLING *TWILIGHT*, *NEW MOON*, AND *ECLIPSE*

Stephenie Meyer's Twilight saga novels have sold over 100 million copies worldwide.

The origins of Jacob Black

Originally, author Stephenie Meyer created the character of Jacob Black to be Bella's friend in *Twilight*. His role was to help Bella learn Edward's secret. But he was given a bigger part in *New Moon*. "From the very beginning, even when Jacob only appeared in chapter six of *Twilight*, he was so *alive*," Meyer wrote on her website. "I couldn't keep him locked inside a tiny role."

Teenage girls adored Taylor as Jacob Black.

jacob

twilight

Filming for *Twilight* began in February 2008. Taylor looked just as Jacob was described in the books. However, his long hair was actually an itchy wig. Taylor hated wearing it. The wig caused problems too. Every time it got caught in Taylor's mouth or eyes, they would have to start the scene again. The weather was also a challenge. Freezing rain and fierce winds made outdoor scenes unbearable.

The strangest thing Taylor had to get used to was instant fame. Jacob already had thousands of adoring fans, who had fallen in love with the character in Stephenie Meyer's books. Taylor said, "I think the fans would love anybody who played Jacob... I'm just lucky to be the one who got the chance."

Three months before *Twilight* hit cinemas, Taylor dropped in at a bookshop near his home. The shop was hosting a midnight release party for the final book in the Twilight saga, *Breaking Dawn*. Nobody knew Taylor would be there. He didn't even tell his **agent**. Word spread, and more than 1,000 girls flocked to the shop to get a glimpse of Jacob Black. Taylor stayed until 2.00 a.m., signing autographs and posing for pictures. He wanted to make sure every girl left happy.

" ... I'd look at myself in the mirror and I wouldn't even be able to recognize myself. It was so weird just to see that hair on me. ... it was very itchy, hot, whatever, annoying."

Taylor on wearing a wig for his role as Jacob Black

Twilight rocks the world

When filming finished, Taylor and the rest of the cast toured the world to promote *Twilight*. Thousands of fans gathered at every venue. At the **premiere** in November 2008, Taylor was in demand. He carried out dozens of interviews.

Finally, Taylor walked the red carpet in a designer suit. He posed for photos with his co-stars, Robert Pattinson and Kristen Stewart. The film was a huge success. US fans spent more than £43 million on tickets in the first weekend, breaking box office records. Robert and Kristen were immediately signed up to work on the sequel, *New Moon*. To his shock, Taylor was not.

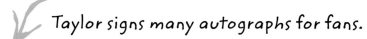

Taylor signs many autographs for fans.

Taylor took a new screen test with Kristen to prove they had Jacob and Bella's chemistry.

New Moon rises

Jacob goes through a lot of changes in *New Moon*. He starts the story as a skinny, carefree boy, and ends it as a huge, muscled werewolf with adult problems. **Producers** were not convinced that Taylor could make these changes to his body and mind.

Taylor knew he could do it, and he fought for the part. He worked out at the gym, cut out junk foods and ate lots of protein-packed meals, such as meat, sweet potatoes, and almonds. He gained 14 kilograms (30 pounds) of lean muscle. Even co-star Robert was envious of Jacob's new look. After another screen test, Taylor won back his role.

CHAPTER 4

Lights on Taylor

New Moon started filming in March 2009. The weather was even worse than it had been for the first film, but Taylor had a brilliant time. He peformed almost all of his own stunts, which included jumping out of a window, climbing a house, and leaping across fields. In this film, he even got to ditch the wig!

Team Taylor

In *New Moon*, Bella has to choose between Jacob and Edward. So do Twilight fans. 'Twi-hards' took sides, joining either 'Team Edward' or 'Team Jacob'. Taylor's role in *New Moon* changed the minds of some 'Team Edward' fans.

Taylor explained how to choose your Twilight 'team' to *MTV*

"[If] you develop this deep friendship and then all of a sudden fall in love later on, then you should be Team Jacob. Come to the dark side. But if you believe in love at first sight and seeing that mysterious man in the corner, then all right, join Team Edward."

When *New Moon* was released, reviews said that Taylor's ripped muscles and powerful acting almost stole the film.

the twilight saga
new moon
11.20.09

It was strange for Taylor to see T-shirts, hats, and even underwear printed with 'Team Jacob' or 'Team Taylor'. Fans even asked Taylor to growl like a werewolf. After agreeing once, he vowed to never do it again.

Taylor loved his beefed-up body and role. But it came with a price. The media followed him everywhere. "Honestly, I try and stay away from what's been written about me, because if you let that stuff get to you, and when it's not true, it can drive you crazy," Taylor said in an interview. To get away from the attention while filming *New Moon*, he hid out at a pensioners' bowling alley!

Taylor's character, Jacob, struggles with his feelings for Bella in *Eclipse*.

Total Eclipse

Even before the release of *New Moon*, cast and crew were working on the third Twilight film: *Eclipse*. This time there was no question who would play Jacob. *Eclipse* has more action, humour, and romance than the first two Twilight films. It is Taylor's favourite book of the series.

Filming for *Eclipse* began in August 2009 and **wrapped** in late October. It was a tough time for Taylor, who had to film scenes without a shirt on, in the freezing cold. At the June 2010 **premiere**, thousands of fans chanted Taylor's name as he walked the specially-made black carpet. He admitted that the screaming fans made him nervous.

Breaking Dawn

Once promotion for *Eclipse* was over, it was time to start preparing for the final films in the Twlight saga. *Breaking Dawn Part 1* (2011) and *Part 2* (2012) feature Taylor even more than the previous films. A big chunk of the story is told from Jacob's point of view.

"I'm having the time of my life, so it couldn't be a better end to my teenage years."

Taylor on filming the Twilight saga

Taylor flew to South America, Asia, and Europe to promote the Twilight films.

CHAPTER 5

An action-packed future!

Taylor's role in the Twilight saga made him a megastar. Like his co-stars Robert and Kristen, he is a regular on magazine covers and TV chatshows around the world. No matter how famous Taylor gets, he remains polite, friendly, and mature. He finds it easy to speak to reporters. His warm personality has earned him the admiration of the public.

Taylor is also one of the hardest-working stars in Hollywood. In July 2009, he had a break between filming *New Moon* and *Eclipse*. Instead of relaxing, he took a role in the romantic comedy *Valentine's Day* (2010), playing a star athlete.

"The thing I love is that my home life hasn't changed. I still help out with the garbage. I still help out with the lawn."

Taylor on still living at home with his family, in an interview with *GQ Magazine*, July 2010

Taylor performed his own stunts in the action film *Abduction*.

Taylor and his father, Daniel, have also entered the filmmaking world as **producers**. The first film that Tailor Made Entertainment worked on was *Abduction* (2011), an action film starring Taylor. More than 900 people turned up to an **open casting call** for extras. Many of them were Twilight fans desperate to share a **set** with Taylor.

Taylor's co-star in *Abduction* is Lily Collins. When Lily was spotted visiting Taylor on the *Breaking Dawn* set, magazines and Internet message boards filled with rumours that they had been secretly dating for months.

producer a person who makes films

In February 2011, *Vanity Fair* magazine revealed that Taylor was out-earning his *Twilight* co-stars. Taylor's hard work helped him become not only the best-paid teenager in Hollywood, but one of the ten highest earners of any age!

Taylor has always wanted to be an action star. It's no surprise that he chose to follow the Twilight saga with exciting, stunt-packed roles. *Incarceron* is based on Catherine Fisher's book for young adults, and will see Taylor escape from a futuristic prison. Tailor Made Entertainment are also producing *Cancun*, a kidnap film that gives Taylor a chance to show off his martial arts skills. His athletic body made him the obvious choice to play the lead in *Stretch Armstrong*, a film based on the best-selling superhero toy.

Just a few years after his career began, Taylor has his choice of high-profile parts. When *Transformers* director Michael Bay decided to team up with Taylor for his next action film, it was headline news. Taylor's biggest challenge will be finding time in his packed schedule to shoot all of the films.

Abduction was Taylor's first leading role.

Taylor is looking forward to life after Twilight.

"It's kind of a gut instinct. It's whatever I'd want to watch. ... It's all based on story and the character. I want to challenge myself to do many different things. I definitely don't want to stay on one road, so I try to change it up."

Taylor on how he chooses his roles, in an interview with *Film.com*

Glossary

agent someone who helps actors find work

ancestors family members who lived long ago

audition a performance given by an actor when he or she is trying out for a part

choreograph to design or plan a series of movements in a dance or other display

open casting call an audition where anyone is allowed to try out

premiere the first public showing of a film

producer a person who makes films

set the stage or scenery for a play or film

stunt double someone who performs action scenes in place of an actor

take the filming of a TV or film scene

wrap complete filming; a word used to signal the end of filming

Find out more

Books

10 Things You Need to Know About Being Famous, Jen Jones (Capstone Press, 2008)

Taylor Lautner: Twilight Star (Young and Famous), Maggie Murphy (PowerKids Press, 2011)

Taylor Lautner: Inside Out, Mel Williams (Piccadilly Press, 2009)

Websites

Get the latest Taylor news, photos and gossip at his fansites, such as:
taylorlautner.org/

Find plots, photographs and quotes from Taylor's latest film projects on his Internet Movie Database page:
www.imdb.com/name/nm1210124/

Fans of Taylor as Jacob Black will like the Twilight fan site **thetwilightsaga.com** and the offical film website **www.twilightthemovie.com**

Check out young Taylor performing his world-beating karate moves at:

www.youtube.com/watch?v=Xa7SqQYGCcg

Index

www.raintreepublishers.co.uk
Visit our website to find out
more information about
Raintree books.

To order:

☎ Phone 0845 6044371
▤ Fax +44 (0) 1865 312263
▣ Email myorders@raintreepublishers.co.uk

Customers from outside the UK please telephone +44 1865 312262

Raintree is an imprint of Capstone Global Library Limited, a company incorporated in England and Wales having its registered office at 7 Pilgrim Street, London, EC4V 6LB – Registered company number: 6695582

Editors: Mari Bolte and John-Paul Wilkins
Designer: Joanna Hinton-Malivoire
Media Researchers: Marcie Spence and Tracy Cummins
Production Specialist: Laura Manthe and Eirian Griffiths
Originated by Capstone Global Library Ltd
Printed and bound in China by Leo Paper Products Ltd

ISBN 978 1 406 22954 7 (paperback)
15 14 13 12 11
10 9 8 7 6 5 4 3 2 1

British Library Cataloguing in Publication Data
Llanas, Sheila Griffin, 1958-
Taylor Lautner. – (Star biographies)
791.4'3'028'092-dc22
A full catalogue record for this book is available from the British Library.

Acknowledgements
AP Images/Vince Bucci/PictureGroup, cover; Alamy/Photos 12; DZilla/BauerGriffin, 5; Capital Pictures, 23; Getty Images/Brad Barket, 17; Getty Images/Vince Bucci, 18; Globe Photos/Nina Prommer, 13; Johnstone/ Raishbrook/Splash News, 7; Newscom, 20, 21, 28; Newscom/Imprint Entertainment/Maverick Films/Summit Entertainment, 16; Newscom/PacificCoastNews, 27; Newscom/SUMMIT ENTERTAINMENT/TEMPLE HILL ENT/ MAVERICK FILMS/IMPRINT/Album, 24; Rex Features/Alex J. Berliner/BEImages, 25; Rex Features/Charles Sykes, cover, 29; Rex USA/Jim Smeal/BEImages, 10; Rex USA/Picture Perfect, 15; SportMartialArts.com, 9.

We would like to thank Isabel Thomas for her invaluable help in the preparation of this book.

Some words appear in bold, **like this**. They are explained at the bottom of the page, or in the glossary.

by Sheila Griffin Llanas